Company in the
Still Dark

Company in the Still Dark

A Gathering of Poetry

M. L. Triplett

Copyright © 2023 M. L. Triplett
triplettm217@gmail.com

ISBN 979-8-218-09995-4

Edited and designed by Tell Tell Poetry

Printed in the United States of America

First Printing, 2023

To my sister

Abstract

These poems, which have accompanied me through the different aspects of life, occur in the Still Dark or during a turning point that reveals a change from night to day, sadness to questioning, and myriad other transformations.

Contents

First Fig

My candle burns at both ends;
  It will not last the night;
But ah, my foes, and oh, my friends—
  It gives a lovely light!

Edna St. Vincent Millay—
known to family and friends as Vincent.

Company in the Still Dark

On January 30, 2020, the World Health Organization declared the COVID-19 outbreak a public health emergency of international concern.

The Ebbing Flow of Night
Life in the Still Dark

In the dead of night sounds the *whooo whooo* of an owl!
Alone, upon hearing the question *who?*, I chortle.
Through the dimness, the aroma of magnolias rises.
The moon's face, sitting quietly, is elegant.
Immersed in the existence that surrounds me, we breathe in
the midst of the late and empty hour. Creation breathes.
Even alone, my voice rings out loudly as I speak.
My cat, a rescue, wanders by. Her steps, feral.
I feel cocooned, deep and covert, in the atmosphere.
The moon's rays, photons twirling, gleam
through windowpanes. Shortly the dawn
will break, igniting the imagination.
Arduous, the constant changing of the night.
The sun comes and a whole night lies down,
slumbering like a tiger.

Company in the Still Dark

The crowded gloaming

Pressing against me, the beauty.
Filling a green water bottle, the sunshine.
Raising a positive vibration, the music.

Once alone, no awareness of contact.
Blissfully thriving, ignorant of the threat.
Encased by oceans, warnings go unheeded.

Contagious: a multitude waits in the twilight.
What could be worse? No earth,
no stars, no blooms, no tiny birds.

In the Still Dark, company in flocks.
Somewhere in the stratosphere, friends.
Nowhere between us, a feeling of contact.

In a race that has taken all our belongings,
until we are in the nothing, we are lost.
Nowhere is the place it all begins.

All signs of familiarity have risen.
In the still dark, company in flocks.
Like a theme in a fugue, lives enter and exit.

Still Life with Mourning Doves

Universal company suffering

The crickets are singing Mass
without wafers or wine,
in a world of no touching.

The broken-apart parts,
spilling out of a pocket,
too small to hold them all,

flow into the locus of life,
while we all sleep through
the deep black still night.

The dove coos at dawn
with those who have gone on
to wake their loves.

We place our feet
on the sharp shells
on the ocean floor

and, rising, stand in the sun
in the wake of a turbulent
wave that caught us
unaware.

Care feels so much.
Here, there, and everywhere,
someone mourns.

Traveling Annulled

Home alone while the virus takes it all

No new town.
No new house.
No new love.

One new car.
It does not take me far.
From here to there and back.

When the day goes maroon,
travel does not pay.
I am the tree
my things are nesting in.

I am too tired to try;
the sun orbits anyway.
Sinking into dusk, I reach
rare relief in the spent day.

Holiness is a spiral
filling nothing as it
spins before us

into the afterlife.
Walking on the water's surface,
I refuse to dive.

An amphibious insect with no past or future,
I avoid being devoured

by the present.
All alone in this land
of myriad beings, my moment

has come and gone.
Into the never known before,
into the backlit life that turns on its own.

Who's There

Who's company at home?

A bird sings above me
as I look up from the gate
to see his beak open,
pouring a triple twitter
as his chest puffs
with each measure.

I stood anointed,
embraced by the nature
of a Carolina wren.

My head bent slightly
entering the house again
to greet the singular
quietness of quarantine.

My home, a panorama
of daylight filled with
possibilities unimpeded
by company.

A waystation for phone
calls, emails, and texts
turning any second into
a receptacle of Sirius
songs. Sometimes I just sit,
turn pages, and look outside.

Often I think I see someone
appear on the lawn or move past
the window only to dissipate
in my direct gaze.

I wonder what peoples lived
on this land before me, maybe
centuries ago. Connected through
this block of Universe, their songs
resonate as the lyrics change
with each landscape.

Love Poem

Looking for online dating company

Tripping in the light fantastic,
I fall laughing
and spread my limbs
in the golden
ecstasy.

Pulling myself up
by the sternum,
my arms follow my breasts
as I am lifted up

into your love. Standing
in the shining, emanating
everything, by you,
for you, with you

I love. My heart,
a majestic tree, makes
room in its branches for
tonight's twirling winds.

And I change not
in the midst of reinvention:
I am already yours,
rejoicing in the new ours.

The Female Organs of a Flower

Intimate company blooming

Traveling up through
deep black soil
you pulled forth
my pistols

with crystalline embers
shed by your passing
breath.

Our dreams might
populate somes' stigma.
Even so we soar

with style. You
have left your
pollen in my

ovaries, swollen with
new life. I'll burst
over you in

cascading colors.
My passion, spilling
generously, fertilizes
your heart.

Something Is Missing at Seventy

Missing company in curves

When I gaze at the clouds, I see the curves of a
woman.

Darkness, ribbon-like, runs slowly through my
body.

I do not know where it is coming from. Will I
know the intimate love of a woman again?

Wearing my watch and reading Sylvia Plath,
I am waiting: have I had my last chance?

Heaven's Skin

Company in flesh

Star tissue, sun tissue,
the marrow of the night.
Does only earth have flesh?

Tight, fibrous, smooth muscles in youth,
slack, loose fibers with age.
Is there a character to flesh?

A porous, morphing translucence
born in a brooding shrug.
Will I be lonely without my flesh?

This Love Built of Breadcrumbs
Company with poem lovers

The bread, broken,
        spills crumbs
falling between cracks

and behind sofas. The crumbs
        in search for a like heart.
This love built of breadcrumbs

must somehow
        beat in time with a poem
that speaks to a reader

never seen before.
        Floating from another
piece of the loaf,

crumbs fall haphazardly,
        making efforts to form
the dawn of a poem

in the placid mind
        that doesn't care to eat

until it tastes the fruit
        of a wild cherry
in subterranean winter.

How Many Ways of "Passing"?

The company of thorns

She was the only Black female
preacher present at the Universal
Christ convention in Santa Fe.
Her body language punctuated her sermons.

She stopped and bumped her hip
as she ushered my gay hurts—
the pain of social, religious, and familial
rejection—into the Body of Christ.

Flames of love burst in my heart
burning away my luggage of wounds.
At the airport, I sat beside her,
turned toward her, and

told how my soul had changed.
Her energy gorgeously flowed
with Christ's love for me.
Then she said, "It hurts to be Black."

A filigree of twining veins
flowed from a bead of blood
in the white of her brown eye.
Her beautiful brown skin
gave her no way to "pass."

She, a descendent of the raped,
met a descendent of the rapists.
How long had my white history

oppressed her? And to this day,
micro aggressions beat against her being.

My gay history is dotted with tiny
and huge hurts. "Passing" is a straightjacket
at work, at school, as a debutante,
as a church-choir member.

What if the color of my skin revealed
those who are "Gay Like Me"? Historical
clouds covering clandestine injuries lifted . . .
gender, another deep complication of being human.

Can we be authentic: Black children in a white world,
southerners whose forefathers owned slaves, blue stars in a
    red state,
poets living with rejection, divorced parents splitting their
    families,
homeless brothers and sisters, disabled veterans once warriors?

At seventy years old, I am still pulling
out thorns of my "passed," raising
drops of blood, deep red rose buds
that reveal: my real parts.

From Poetry Therapy
Zoom Class Prompts

Introductions at My Four Elements Dinner Party

Company with a haibun
(prose poem followed by a haiku)

My name is resilience. I find
I bounce back from difficult
situations over and over.

My name is brokenness. My being
is filled with healed stem tips
budding where the breaks occurred.

My name is crystal. No color, shape,
transparency, or power alone can define
me. I come as a single stone with multiple facets.

My name is mood. I live mostly in
the heart and the car. I'm known
as up, down, madness, and sanity.

This resilience—
finds a path through brokenness
wearing crystal moods.

Life Like Heat Waves on Hot Asphalt
A company of thoughts

Goodnight took 'til sunup.
Our first kiss, kindled
in pinpoint laser-like stars,
mingled all night 'til dawn.

My ancestors live in my black hair.
Black hair crowns my mother's mother,
tow-headed at birth.
Is gray hair our souls evolving?

Have mild COPD after five years.
Air sacs deep in my lungs
refuse to collapse, as if I didn't
smoke but swam for forty years.

Told to cycle instead of walk for exercise.
Bent arthritic toes carry
with flexible willingness
my strolling gait down morning lanes.

I fell in love with a romantic scammer.
I rub my broken hearts together,
taste their moist red skin,
and believe in myself again.

Told surgery would clear up my sight.
My eyes fog until cataracts,
trying to crowd pure sight,
roll back with blinking.

The ageless mother inside a childless woman.
My modest breasts,
nipples full of my eternal
baby's milk, ache with love.

Coconut Cake with Ice Picks

Company of scents

The last time I saw you,
I could not smell the anger
that rose from your sorrow,
and I was utterly unprepared.

I walked out the patio door,
not speaking, and stopped
beside the tea olive.

Its fragrance
overcame the moment with sweetness
like no other flower's scent
filled my nostrils before it.

Your laughter rang from inside
and it reminded me of childhood.
How quickly your chuckle erased
my tear, unfolding a posy smile.

Scents of lavender and the lilies
of the valley soothed my rattled
nerves, and then I was prepared
to see you again.

Brown-Eyed Angels Sit with Me

Company mentally in words

Brown-eyed angels sit with me,
holding me as I age while syllables fly
away to realms beyond recall
(the noetic loss of inimitable shells).

Words may elude conscious thought,
yet every experience inhabits
the persistence of recollections. The last
stage of life finds wholeness in community.

Memories come pre-packed
with the words needed to describe
life from long before
as if it were here now.

Poems Written in Scotland

Arbroath

Company with poets touring

Small Scottish town
        in the summer by the sea
whose smoked-fish aroma
        seeps into the sides of the tour bus.

Through the old town
I stroll expectantly,
my cheeks turn red,
furrows appear on my forehead.

The group meets for dinner
at the end of the street.
Watching the blue firth of Tay,
still and flat offshore,

we inhale in wonder the Scottish zephyr.
The sun sparkles like glitter on
the surface of the Tay as my eyes
gradually draw back to shore.

Unlike the locals, some tourists
        eat their meals
on the beach, and seagulls
        steal snacks from their plates.

My salivary glands ache
        with the juices
generated when dining
        at the Golden Haddock.

We dine at the Golden Haddock
savoring the moist, firm taste
of the local catch, fresh from sea to table.

My American ears tickle
        with unfamiliar Scottish burrs
which sound like green grass bending
        and toothpicks clicking.

Now we smell like smoked fish
        as we file into the bus
and collapse to sit quietly,
        crossing the firth of Tay.

Edinburgh

Ghosts keeping company

My ghosts have lived here longer than I have.
I walk around in bones stepping on bones
left by the dead. My ghosts permeate me
with renewal. If only they would speak louder.
I hear them singing in the air blowers.
With ghostly resonation, my heart tunes in.
When I cross over, my ghosts will join
my future ghost and leave their haunting
places for a new birthplace: somewhere
fresh and unknown; maybe crowded
with ancestors taking ghostly strolls
amongst the descendants. The night
draws us magnetically upward so we
can replenish our stardust.

Notions of Dundee Scotland

Poems accompany travelers

The tap water flowed down
from the mountains.
I took a water bottle with me
everywhere. My writing
pad, folder, and pens
tucked in my backpack.

The penetrating light shone
as if we were in high heaven,
sitting by the window
in the dining room. A pleasant
peace descended as we were
served with a Scottish brogue
the celebratory meal in three
courses, each carrying cuisine
in Dundee's unfamiliar wrapping.

Windows tilting out into the night
allowed cool dry air into the tiny room.
I lay on my back on the bed; the seagull
squawks sounded like broken bits of human
voices conversing, flying by
the fifth story window
then away over the firth
of Tay.

Nine writers gathered,
each reading recent
heartfelt expression

sharing what was later
an intimate vulnerability.
Astonishing, the depth
of transfer with strangers
morphs into soul travel
in a foreign country.
Each traveling with her own
story that becomes part of mine.

Onion Skin Is the Membrane on a Layer

Company with grief in Dundee

Cut in half, the white onion's
wet layers drip a liquid
that burns the tongue.

My grief so fresh, new
and young in the kitchen
chopping with Mama.

Eating a thick slice of white onion
on a hamburger, my grief outlasts the meal
in strong, pungent breath.

My sorrow in middle age
seeps slower and softer.
An edgy mildness tastes
like purple onions in salad.

Seeing my shadow in the cave
after sixty years of darkness,
I chew, digest, and swallow
forgiveness.

Lamentations emerge
in labile feelings
and subside like a vapor,
not lingering in the breath.

Place

Southern company in Scotland

In the Deep South
　　　　aromatic snow-encrusted gardenias
　　　　cause another inhale,
　　　　humidity like wet sheets
　　　　feels like trouble breathing.

Greetings disguise the subtle
　　　　privilege of complicity.

Consciously loving the unconscious
　　　　breaks the heart.

Place and kindred entwine
　　　　through history's stretching tissue,

wrapping the way it always was
　　　　in a kaleidoscope of colors.

Sunrise refracts rainbows
　　　　above the morning dew.

The journey, a jewel crafted
　　　　by each one's trembling hand.

My next birthplace,
　　　　another continent.

My essence,
　　　　gardenias.

Ten Thousand Steps

Empty dorm room after poetry class

maybe twenty,
between meetings
into the evening.

I return
to my monastic place,
a gathering space,
spare and simple.

Greeted by a hot room,
my camouflaged emptiness
rises to the surface.

I didn't know I could love
a cat so much.
She talks and meditates,
curls up on me
and naps alone.

I didn't know I loved
ice in my nose hairs
at six thousand feet
under Pike's Peak
walking in a down vest
through the pouring down snow.

I know I didn't love
spending time on psychiatric
wards not once
but three times.

I knew three institutional
         directors who thought
supper at home
         was a fun way
to leave behind
         the haunting faces
of the demented.

Night-time

When Half-Spent Was the Night
Life in the Still Dark

The stars, a rash of pinpoints,
penetrate the velvet black dome.
The trees, like the King's guards,
stand in a night crawling with creatures.

The owl, a rare Bloom, appears
beneath the window of the living room.
The hooting, like a bass drum beating,
captures the occupants dreaming.

The thought, a repeated note, carries
the melody from day into night.
The darkness, like an untamed wildness,
surrounds a Presence.

The mind, a blinking constellation,
moves slowly into new Awareness.
The heart, like a ticking clock,
notices the Passions that ripple within.

The Manger, an outsider's crib,
shares its space with the sheep.
The Season, like a cold bath,
seeps across the countryside.

The star, a clairvoyant crystal,
leads Wise Men with second sight.
The Birth, like an inheritance from angels,
spins an intricate web of hope.

A Heavenly Rendezvous

Company beyond the night

Laughter radiates from my father
and brother surrounding me
with great happiness and promises
of a beautiful life.

Pleasure pulses ride my bloodstream
through weightless veins and arteries.
Slowly my dull tendrils turn pale green
and curl around my once sobbing heart.

Configurations of stone beaming green
reside upon my heart. With a healing touch,
my soul wakes up with my loved ones
again and again and again.

We know very well where we are,
in lawn chairs on the green earth beside
the Pawley's Island hammock.
Now a site for visitors from heaven.

Jesus and Buddha and Fred and Pop.
They're always a few feet from us,
especially within the constellations
of our interior.

House Hunting (3)

Reflective company in the Still Dark

The city is sleeping. I am not.
Darkness covers the gentle profile of mountains.
Streetlights shutterclick like fractured beams.

I am in the nowhere between there and here.

The hotel is a liminal space.
Before I move into the mountains.
Before I leave the piedmont.

My gauzy reflection looks like a ghost in the window.

Once black like the patches of darkness between city lights,
my gray hair is bedhead soft, mussed
like my sister walked by and messed my hair.

I slip into the ease of being with night in the evening of
    unknowing
and the evening of long past dusk, dawn nowhere near.

Waiting without wanting while sleep escapes me.

A transparent figure floating in the window
is my body filled with mountain peaks and valleys.

This moment I am alive.

Some higher consciousness breathes me regularly.
It is my intersection with eternity.

Up and Down

The Hairy Green Caterpillar
Price of dawn's company

Transitive the transformation from child
to blossoming girl. My petals blew in the wind
in a peculiar fashion. Unbecoming according
to stereotypical Southern role models:

inappropriate and a silence that spoke
loud disdain for what was expected.
After jumping over and over from a hill
into the soft red mud, I wore the jeans

covered in orange earth into the house.
Stopping in terror upon seeing my piano
teacher, of all people, sitting in the living room,
I slid in shame upstairs to change from a moment

of great fun to my role of civility. A spoke
grew from the rim of my life to my heart.
Scolding and chiding, it connected all
happiness at a remarkably high cost.

Upon Hearing Bach

Notes in company

In a twelve-year-old heart, I play
piano—a Bach prelude—in junior high
for assembly. Expecting adolescent derision,
the wild clapping sounds astound me.

As my fingers do a deep trot-trot
on the keys, my soul unravels,
exposing my heart in the keyboard
encased in shiny, black wood.

I am without flesh, the celestial harmony
my only body. A black five-line double
staff winds over hilltops in clouds,
filling my fingertips with notes.

As if I were Goldberg playing
the aria and thirty variations
for the first time with a spirit in
thirty-one dimensions.

Or, as if hearing Bach presented
to Brandenburg. My viscera flutters,
sending vicissitudes that shift
the direction of my heart

into heaven when a cello's horsehair
bow pulls back. The note suspended
until suddenly—like a strangled stream
let loose, I loved and loved and loved.

The Inches We Share

Company standing on a ruler

Residual layers, pressed down,
carried for lifetimes, rise and fly
on gossamer wings, leaving no
trails, but followed by
unsuspected older issues,
buried, wrinkled, and crinkled.

It's the undoing of patterns
woven in flesh and spirit
released as their texture
is changed by white light.

My body—like a medium
exuding ectoplasm—is the true me,

truly rising from the field between
this and that, old and new, whole and wounded,
chaos and rigidity, punctured and patched,
faithful and false.

Could I ever more deeply feel,
in the red rosin of the horsehair
bowstring, the vibration's design
filling every valley, every peak
in my irregular existence?

A crowd of spirits stand
all at once on a ruler. The inches
we share described in genealogies,
old photos, and Shakespeare's sonnets.

Mingling transcends convention:
a White Aborigine,
a Buddhist Viking.
a Greek Oriental.

We wind the future
like vines plumbed
and dense with orchards.

Leads in My Heart

Company with a pacemaker

In the time of my deception,
a flock of unruly passions unfolds,
a fantasy imprisons my mind.

I look for a way out
through imagined pathways.
Consumed by lack of sleep,

my eyes open and close
like shutters weathered and old.
I cannot accept the weakness

in the floor of my being.
A life that is peeling away.
Loneliness is my bedside table.

How inadequate my attempts
to find new connections. They
disappear with the stars at dawn.

How unruly could passions be
when no one is there?
The clouds hide the moon.

With toothpicks for eyelids,
I stare into the wee hours
of the night, tormented.

Carousel images from years ago
flash in my brain, like slides on a screen.
Those who appear, no longer living.

Measures of a song drift
toward resolution with finite steps
toward all conclusions. Escape

drops me, temporal and empty.
I have everywhere to go
and no way to get there.

The Callous Association
Past company betrayal

She wore a sterling silver
        diamond-cut rope necklace.
The metallic adornment clanged
        against her brassy heart.
Her eyes, heavy-lidded and dark,
        ferret out her latest fascination
like telescopes magnifying her victim.

She takes no prisoners, the last morsel
        of appearances ingested thoughtlessly.
Lacking empathy, she strives for the taken,
        the owned, cast-aside, or pedestal high.
Her encounters shiver in her presence
        and turn toward avenues of escape,
already trapped in passive self-annihilation.

She guards against any sliver of recognition;
        her instincts are to externalize.
We have all known someone like her,
        from our childhood, from our dreams,
from our own disarming self.
        Though uncommon, she is present
in the turmoil, the tiny twisting of life.

She makes a special trip
        to my workplace after returning
from Europe to let me know she
        never wants to see me again.
I am glad to see her, then quickly adjust

my mask to hide a stricken
soul, shocked but not surprised.

So that was that, the snake's tongue
        unfurled and withdrawn, never revealing
the fangs: they were already embedded
        deep in my heart. With a cut
so sharp and thin that thought
        did not enter in, concealed already
from who I knew she was.

Declining with Dementia

To Whom the Goodness Comes

A few months before my mother went to hospice

My ninety-year-old mother
likes to sleep late and watch

TV in bed in the morning.
The nurses say it is ok

to be a late riser. My heart
is warm knowing she is where

she can do her thing. She chats
and eats and smiles, laughing

to herself. I have not always
been so free to love her.

Knowing her for the first
time without all the baggage,

the scabs have fallen off
my wounds, the skin smooth

and soft. Memories play
in a welcome light,

abiding in her faithfulness
to her oldest daughter.

My oldest, deepest love rose
from the ashes of the wounded.

I wouldn't trade any
of my past moments for

another's. Each has their own.
Our DNA shows in long

fingers, good bones,
black eyes, gray hair.

From these the soul
emanates like a setting

sun painting the sky
in reddish variations.

Gifts for an Elderly Mother

The music of the soul, and above all
of great and of feeling souls.—Voltaire

Words enter her mind in a random assortment;
some, filling a thought, leave a dent.

Learning poems by heart in the schoolyard,
her young mind did not find it hard.

Now her memory, fragments filling each hole,
a hole in a sweater that no longer fits her soul.

Dementia is not something that time heals;
it is searching for words that time steals.

When I visit her, I bring her presents,
a warm embrace, a tender word, a presence.

Her words issue from recollections in a sphere
that haphazardly play by ear.

Her muscles are tired as her mind dozes
while the day opens and closes.

All the while, her memory fades
and dims as if lowering shades.

Who jumped over the moon?
What ran away with the spoon?

Lord, Teach Me to Share

Visiting Mom at hospice

I walked into her hospice room
and the bed was elevated
so she could sit up
and eat the fruit from her tray:

big, juicy halves of deep, red
strawberries. I asked her if they
were good and she said they
were all right. She asked me

if I wanted one and I said no.
A few moments later, she
asked me if I wanted a strawberry,
and I said no.

I said no because I didn't want to know
if strawberries that beautiful
did not taste good. Later I felt
a pelt of sadness covering

the puncture from not
sharing with her. When I
left, I cupped her cheek
in my right hand and said,

"You are my special person.
You are the most wonderful
person in the world to me."
First, I thought there was only silence.

Then my mother, with end-stage dementia,
turned to me and said, "That is
something I will never forget."
My heart felt like a strawberry.

The Body of the Planet

Showers of Leaves

The company of autumn

Like a hot branding iron
        burning my cerebellum,

two flaming red oak trees release
        a pair of solar flares that touch the sky,

illuminating a solitary sun-drenched yellow maple tree
        residing nearby.

Slowly, shading and outlines
        return as the colorful glare resolves.

A glance into autumn colors—
        almost blinding.

What epiphany does this bright
        season foretell?

The Disappearing Pine-Woods Sparrow in York County, SC

Company with a disappearing lineage

Streaks down your nape
and over your back
in black and gray,

a stripe over your eye
in rufous brown.
If your markings

were mine, how exquisitely
they would wrap
my pale skin.

But having no feathers,
I would not be
as beautiful as you.

Oh, that I had such
a clear, sweet whistle,
modulating to a trill.

From my home
I hear the degrading
of your habitat.

Your natural world
shredded and torn.
My song is not

strong enough to keep
you safe nesting
in pine tree carpets.

We are both little-known,
occurring nowhere
else in the world.

Your wings beat
in my declining heart
that hopes to hear

your sweet chip-chip
in heaven (sometimes only
three feet away).

Passing Down the Crinum

The least of things with meaning is worth more in life
than the greatest of things without it.—Carl Jung

Fragile, delicate, unseen connection woven like a spider's
web. For years,

in a millisecond, each word, gesture, or look changes
everything. Born

in the same decade, to the same mother, sharing
childhood toys clothes

yards neighbors a brother. A great many unlikely events
happen with

the existence of siblings unfolding after millions of years
going back before

human beings or even hominids: a meeting between
sperm and egg

with a one in 250 million chance for the sperm's
existence. Located

in a galaxy on a life-supporting planet, the survival of
every ancestor to a

reproductive age is exceedingly (but not infinitely) small.
The astonishing

existence of two sisters shining in this generation growing
up on hills

like purple lilacs attracting butterflies might never be told,
but they are still

bold as water lilies returning to waterways after the rain.
  In our childhood

yard, an old home site, the eighteen-inch bulb of the
  crinum shows the passage

of time for decade upon decade. At my sister's, house and
  yard are populated by

the passing down of tables chairs books pictures rugs
  chests and shrubs plant

life and flora. On an ordinary sunny Sunday afternoon,
  sitting in her backyard

watching bees and hummingbirds fly between us to the
  flowers growing behind us,

ideas and convictions exchanged, epiphanies and history
  shared with the transplanted

crinum flourishing outside the fence.

Summer in the Neighborhood
Company without humans

Tiny flying red fuzzy
winged insect flew
around me to get by.
It was flying faster
than I was walking.
The beautiful moving
scarlet tone brought
me back to the present
as I wandered aimlessly
in the morning air.

Awakened from my own hazy
slightly anxious thoughts,
relief filled with snowing
crepe myrtles,
shedding in white,
deep purple, and red.
The wind blew gently
and scattered
the crinkled petals
throughout the wooded area.

Thanks to the furry
red flying bug,
whose name
I do not know,
I was not staring
at my feet, lost
in unpleasant thoughts
of imagined tribulation.

Three or four magnolia trees
line the sidewalk
and the fragrance
of the large milky-white blossoms
greeting me in the spring
dissipates in the wind.

These gentle reminders
of the world going on around us
lifts the spirits as well
as eyes ears and heart
to an earthy plane.

Even the sun shining
on the petals of the hedge,
spreading its crisp
leafy brilliance
throughout its body.

Almost as if a wood nymph
reached inside my chest
to hold my heart and fill it
with the day's grandeur
and changing dimensions.

My mind is winding
its way around in spirals,
shedding bark and
the ancient magnolias.

In the Black, Deep, Heavenly Lit Backyard

Company with my brother who died at
42 years old

We were watching Johnny Carson.
        Everyone else had gone to bed.

My brother said, "Let's go outside."
        I followed barefoot,
           walking in the cold wet grass.

The backyard, an acre, high
        above the town. The darkness
        covered us like a cloak.

Then we lifted our heads skyward.
        Silver stars studded
        the inky blackness.

In between the Big Dipper
        and the Little Dipper,
        Draco, the Dragon, a long,
        winding, dim constellation.

The star maps went deeper
        and deeper into the night,
        winking from lightyears away.

We stood entranced, heads craned back,
        absorbed into the darkness
        of the night and the wonder
        of the celestial bodies.

Finding Oneself

Past Times

Company at a family feast

A tall magnolia tree
surrounded by ancient boxwood
lives in the front yard.
I want to bring in a bloom.

Profound, velvet, white petals
with large, waxy, green leaves
float in a silver tray.

The table is set with fine china
around the blossom. We bring
red and rings of gold and silver
to the dining room repast.

The sideboard is set with trays
and ceramic squares to protect it
from hot casseroles and dishes.
The meat is carved in the kitchen.

The imminence of the meal
is punctuated by the pouring
of the mint tea. The biscuits
are still in the oven.

We gather into an ancestral line.
Picking up plates, we choose
from the luscious buffet
of favorite seasonal recipes.

Small talk, eating, and drinking.
But first bring the hot biscuits
and pass the butter. Nodding,
we agree: this is good.

Where I'm From

Original company

I am from honeysuckle
        juice sweet on the tongue.

I am from next door to two old ladies
        with we never knew how many cats.

I am from a playground
        across the street with giant swings
        and seesaws that left splinters.

I am from a slow walk around the block
        my tiny hand in her beautiful black hand.

I am from morning thunderstorms and galoshes
        and rain gear dripping in the cloak room.

I am from shouting and diving and running
        through the grass with a bee sting on my foot
        covered by a tobacco plug
        wet with my father's spit.

I am from excitement on the way to the pool
        riding my bike into the bushes missing the
        sharp downhill turn.

I am from racing home dragging my best friend
        to see my new baby sister in the crib
        with a crown of soft black hair.

I am from fresh lemons squeezed and floating in
        sugar water, drinking glasses in the backyard,
        the green pitcher, and me sweating.

I am from all places southern: tea olive, fig
        bushes, purple iris, and tall pecan trees.

I am from all people southern: breathing their air,
        climbing their trees, gazing at their stars.

I am from the future feeling grand and small
        and young and old, haunted by the
        emotional contradictions of my Southerness.

The add-a-pearl necklace
Company with old-time gift

Sixty years old, draped
across the palm of my hand,
jogs Christmas memories
marching through my mind,
a ghostly band.

Dying of Alzheimers after ten years,
she gave me my first pearl and two
smaller each Christmas after.
This young girl thought some
other gift would be better—
a toy or a sweater.

Other gifts are gone with the years.
But here are eleven tiny pearls
on a tiny gold chain necklace
holding the fragrance, the laughter,
brightly glinting in ivory whirls.

Pleated skirts and drinks and popcorn
on the fire, grandparents, aunts
and uncles, my cousins yet to be,
gather toasting by the Christmas tree.
Spirits gone leaving none to be born.

I see them through the pearls,
each milky albumen shining,
assuring love is not waning
but trembling between the worlds.

Blue Moon

Company with rare events

The third full moon
        in a season
that has four full moons:
        is the moon ever really blue?

Eruption of Krakatoa
        in 1883 caused a blue moon
all over the Earth
        for nearly two years.

Once in a blue moon
        an owl hoots outside.
Once in a blue moon
        Congress votes for universal health care.
Once in a blue moon
        a red fox crosses the road.
Once in a blue moon
        an egg has a double yolk.
Once in a blue moon
        we skip church.
Once in a blue moon
        Bowie's *Let's Dance* plays.
Once in a blue moon
        my spirit guide speaks.
Once in a blue moon
        I do not shake.
Once in a blue moon
        there is no war.

Once in a blue moon
     I read Emily Dickinson.
Once in a blue moon
     no animals are slaughtered.
Once in a blue moon
     gays and conservatives embrace.
Once in a blue moon
     a US president is impeached.
Once in a blue moon
     I read *The Sacred Universe.*
Once in a blue moon
     I sleep all night for a week.
Once in a blue moon
     the moon is vaguely blue.

When Fitting Means More Than a Fashion
Unfulfilling company work

I was the only woman working with ten self-absorbed
software experts in a start-up company in San Antonio.
Surprised by my intelligence, they counted on failure.
It was like wearing diamond-studded high heels to a
junior high school dance. I escaped from work for ninety
minutes a week with no explanation to take lessons in jazz
piano from all-the-rage Nobuko. Her home was a
layout of white one step up, one step down open areas.
Her Eastern style was calm, creative, and conducive
to change. We sat on the piano bench with no sheets
of music and made interesting sounds come from
unplanned chords and arpeggios. As I prevaricated, she
encouraged me to spin from a note, uphold a tonal cloud
and practice *Autumn Leaves* in every key. I was awestruck
by her ivory magic music. At work, my absence eventually
raised questions. This escape was destined to be short-lived.
But it did not end my search for shoes that fit.

Who Cares Who I Might Have Been

Company with just being myself

We never stay the same. We age and move
and change clothes. We sob and laugh
and forget to write.

I loved you then but you are no more here,
freeing up the space in my heart for angels
escorting new friends.

We meet in the cloud sitting in front of my door.
Never one for crowds, connection comes
through entering the unknown.

Grounded to Mother Earth through my tailbone
eases the shakiness and gives my stomach
a firm foundation.

It is not that I'm not scared, it's just
that fear does not live in this new world.
I am all eyes and ears.

This fifth dimension of happiness
is letting the Universe unfold what
I need today.

Whoever crosses my path is Divine
intervention. Like a bird who sings
a song when I walk by.

Heavenly Themes

Playing Dido & Aeneas

Operatic company

Used to ride my bike at USC
across Columbia to the church.
Spacious and cool inside,
empty and silent. A safe place.

I climbed the stairs to the balcony
to play the organ. There my inside
matched my outside, a voluminous void
with changing weather and sacred icons.

It was a time of seeking and curiosity,
entering a stillness after my move
from one undergraduate school to another,
four times, finally arriving close to home.

Late night practices, I accompanied the
rehearsal of *Dido & Aeneas*: love
and tragedy. Dido, tormented by three witches,
kills herself with Aeneas' sword.

Norman picked me up afterward;
we would go to the Main Street diner
to eat a ham sandwich and drink
several pitchers of beer.

Norman played Ravel's Piano Concerto in G Major,
adagio assai, the slow movement.
That is when we met. He was married and I
was a tormented queer, so we got along fine.

I never had any money but scraped together
enough for a ticket to hear Beverly Sills sing.
I went alone and sat in the high reaches
of the last balcony; she was a tiny figure on the stage.

But her voice, sublime, ornamental,
carried without hindrance to the heights
of the auditorium. Full and vibrato,
the deeps deep, the highs soaring.

Enthusiastic clapping brought two encores,
but when she acquiesced to a third,
I was not prepared for it to be the highlight
of the whole concert. She said it was a lullaby,

an exercise, she learned as a teenager.
A cappella, the legato lifts me
from my seat, the simple evolution,
a butterfly still wet from its caterpillar form.

We were born with her that night
as we heard her enter her vocation,
her true self reveling as her body became
her instrument for musical memories.

Nancy in Heaven

Loved a college friend's company

Planted deep into the earth
of my heart fifty years ago,
I never forgot you.

Even in winter I would till
the soil around your memory
and search for you on Google.

Never finding you, I let you
hibernate with me like two cubs
in a cave with no mother.

Two fragile souls, our fingers
dared not touch for we hid
in the secret places of our time.

From a distance, I asked
were you happy, were you
loved like you needed to be loved?

What brought about your early
departure to heaven? You,
a world away, still grow in me.

Maybe you going closed the distance.
Maybe you know now how much
I love you.

Maybe that's you I feel
moving toward me, shimmering
even though the sun is not shining.

Maybe you heard my shocked
grief and watched the loss
leak through me.

Maybe you know
how much it mattered to me
that you were okay.

The Piano Lamp
Autobiographical company

Autobiographical company evokes an odd sadness in my chest. Long brown steel curved adjustable neck and the horizontal lamp angling over the piano music to shed its covered light. My parents' gift. I was fresh out of university with a piano degree. Then, all was bright and young and full of promise, and dreams were new every day, still years from tarnishing. No plans, a talent, and a heart expectant and conflicted. How could it have painlessly worked out? The discordant voices joined in full force with the themes changing places daily, sometimes hourly: mother, the South, sexuality, financial dependence, anger, bipolar moods, drinking, smoking, acute introversion. Life was short, unstable, and fragile, but something in me was tough.

That is why I gaze at the forty-eight-year-old piano lamp
    sitting on
top of my piano having traveled faithfully by my side even
    when
there was no piano. Assessing the resolution of all that
    strife,
I bow down to an existence in experimental endeavoring.
    My one talent
is surrounded by an unexpected fortune: sanity, sobriety,
    mysticism,
creativity. A room of my own for whatever love brings.
    Waves
cycle over a softening interior, more wiry than tough, with a
    mellowed maturity, a comfort in an aging shell.

Gray haired and entering my prime, after the struggle
  subsides, there
remains what is the best, which can only be seen from
  this vantage point,
after youngness. Sad naive innocence: its going
reveals a tree, bearing leaves and flourishing, twisting
  gently
in the wind, a shade when everything becomes too bright.
Not one moment is to be exchanged. Every blemish
  reveals a
greater source swelling soaring and sailing on into this
  autumn season.

Feeling Lonely in a Crowd
No company in church

Make note of it: the spire that touches the sky
rising over the emptiness of a congregation.
For her, that spire pierces the heart
with its cold, metal, impersonal outline.

Her heart cannot integrate in a church
that hands have built. Some Divine
something indwells her heart like a home.

Her beating beacon seeks out others
whose house is inside,
drawn with a flash of recognition
to gather anywhere, anytime.

Her sanctuary travels in and out
of buildings and cars and parks
and neighborhoods: at the library
reading, at the restaurant eating.

The sky is her ceiling, the earth,
her floor. Her eyes read the vibes
through the lift of an eyebrow
like the tilting of a bird's wing.
Her ears tune to the mood
through the sound of words
like echoes from radar's rebound.

In the most average, everyday moment,
the world dispenses love for pain
and horrors for love.

My God does not ask to be worshipped,
only that my sanctuary embrace
broken steps in a broken world.

Her steps, crossing the crumbling of cruelty
with benevolence, share her natural
surroundings with spires over empty buildings.

Where in the World Are You, Jesus?

Company between Heaven and Earth

I am here

beneath the cross

brushing the dirt from my legs,
smeared with sweat and blood.

Glad that is over with.

What is that in my hair?
Clumps of clotted blood.

The earth has a pulse.
My heart has stopped.

I need no air to breathe.
My thirst is quenched.

Who thought it would be like this?

The women weeping.
The soldiers gambling.
My heart bursting.

Walking is like wading
in a waist-high stream,
no need to be anywhere.

I am here

in the world shaken
by an earthquake.

Silent birds in dusk
that interrupts sunlight.

None of it hurts anymore though
I still have the wounds.

Who will believe this?

I am still at home on earth.

I have not risen from the dead

I am with the dead, wandering.

We appear and disappear.
We know we do not know.

The Fig Sonnet

Improvised company

She leaned into me.
The wind pushed me back.
The glare closed my eyes.
The bird grasped the limb.
The tweet soothed my chills.
The rock warmed my heart.
The stone felt my hand.
The gold cleft the blue.
The horse kept my pain.
The fig hid her face.
The fur wrapped my soul.
The rain drew my sleep.
The star shined so bright.
The night closed the day.

A Thousand Tiny Hearts

Company in the still blaze

A thousand tiny hearts
hang from her branches—scarlet
jewels blazing in the sun.
Crescents of crimson wave in the wind,
climbing all around her.

O that I had a heart so
brilliant, so free on the bough,
riding gracefully atmospheric
oscillations. A heart

rejoicing in the passing
of the day, as sunset pulls down
the shades until the red bud
tree shines in the moonlight.

About M. L. Triplett

M.L. Triplett is a gay poet born in Chester, South Carolina in 1951. She studied at six universities and finally received a Bachelor of Arts degree. She wandered from South Carolina living in several states and pursuing several careers. She returned to South Carolina in 1998 leaving behind friends, partners, creativity, and her sanity. She retired in Tega Cay, South Carolina in 2013 and began to find again her lost love of poetry and music. She lives with her cat in Park Pointe Village in Rock Hill, South Carolina.

www.ingramcontent.com/pod-product-compliance
Lightning Source LLC
Chambersburg PA
CBHW051815040426
42446CB00007B/678